CRYPTO
FOR
STARTERS

Paola Eliahoo

TSL Publications

Disclaimer

The information contained within this book is not financial advice. I am not a financial advisor. Cryptocurrency is a high-risk investment. Be cautious. Everyone in the crypto space is partial, one way or another. Either they are investors, blockchain-based creators or businesses profiting from cryptocurrencies. The crypto News Media are quite changeable, so double check everything.

Published in Great Britain in 2019
By TSL Publications, Rickmansworth

Copyright © 2019 Paola Eliahoo

ISBN: 978-1-912416-68-4

Cover Image: Paola Eliahoo

The right of Paola Eliahoo to be identified as the author of this work has been asserted by the authors in accordance with the UK Copyright, Designs and Patents Act 1988.

Table of Contents

Introduction

Why venture into the wonderful world of cryptocurrencies and blockchain?

If you're reading this book, you heard of cryptocurrencies and want to know more. My interest started with XRP, a cross-border payment and settlement coin. It was brought to my attention by Bill McLellan. He was interested in setting up a peer to peer service for people sending small amounts of money to their families abroad. We were concerned by the devasting effects of the 2008 financial crisis. He came across Ripple Labs and we decided to investigate further. What follows is what I discovered.

The blockchain, which underpins cryptocurrency, is a ground-breaking technology. It has the potential to transform our lives as much as the Internet has, if not more.

This small book will give you an honest appraisal of the state of crypto now, in January 2019. It will show you what to look for in a cryptocurrency start-up, and briefly look at the development of older blockchain technology, like Bitcoin, which is ten years old. The crypto space is still very new, and to some extent, lawless. But that will change.

Bitcoin, Satoshi Nakamoto's invention, gives us ownership of our own money. It's a powerful idea; a secure, digital alternative to cash. In fact, the complex cryptography protocols associated with blockchain can encrypt any kind of data transfer, not just money. It will be used for smart contracts. Anything that requires transparency, accuracy, security and speed. For example, automating the process of buying a house, voting in an election, or claiming on an insurance policy.

For all its potential, cryptocurrency has had its share of problems. 2018 saw a long bear market, the price of coins going steadily down from an all-time high in December 2017. There was the Bitconnect Ponzi scheme, which promised up to 120%

interest when you swapped Bitcoin for the Bitconnect coin. Typical of a Ponzi scheme, it collapsed when there weren't enough new investors to cover the 'interest' payments to the old users.

There were Initial Coin Offering scams, and pump and dump episodes. Pump and dumps occur when a group of investors deliberately buy up a particular coin, to increase the price regardless of how good it is. This encourages other people to buy it. As the price of the coin shoots up, the group dumps their coins all at once, at the higher price. People unaware the coin has been pumped and dumped lose money, because they don't sell in time.

Beware of misinformation. There are real scams, which are fraudulent activities done by criminals, but sometimes people throw the word scam about carelessly. Usually they are invested in a particular coin and publicly trash another competitor coin. There are Bitcoin 'maximalists', who believe that only Bitcoin will succeed, and the same 'maximalist' support applies to lots of other coins.

Enthusiastic individual investors may be put off by what has happened in the last few years, but Wall Street is gearing up to get on board in 2019. Something is stirring.

The terminology is changing too. Cryptocurrencies are now called digital assets, probably to attract big investors from the stock markets, and also because the technology and its purpose has matured.

Despite the bear market, a lot of blockchain infrastructure was built during 2018, which is good news.

Meanwhile, the US Securities Commission are trying to clean up the ICO markets, and those involved in Bitconnect are being sued. You still have to be careful though, because once a bull market returns and prices rise, so will the scammers. There is a list of Youtubers near the end of this book who will alert you to scams, and keep you informed about the crypto world. The market is not mature yet so there will still be volatility in the future.

The crypto space is continuously evolving. If you have any questions you can find me on Twitter:

Crypto For Starters @StartersCrypto

Who to trust? The financial crisis of 2008

The housing markets and rating agencies

The 2008 financial crisis showed us that we couldn't trust some of the people and institutions holding our money.

In the early 2000s investors used the US housing market to earn high returns on interest rates. Financial institutions sold large numbers of shares, containing mortgage-backed securities, to investors. House prices were going up and mortgage lenders were confident they would not lose money. Safe as houses. Credit agencies like Standard & Poor and Moody's gave the securities triple A ratings. The leading agencies controlled 95% of the ratings market. If they said something was good, no one else was likely to contradict them.

Success bred more demand. Lenders lowered their standards, lending to home buyers with poor credit and low incomes. These new buyers received low rates of interest to start with, but those initial rates would soon go up until people couldn't afford to pay them (Horsley, 2007).

The poison spread into other safe havens. Pensions funds and large capital funds are only allowed to buy highly-rated securities. The credit agencies misinformed them.

Cue the bubble. People couldn't keep up with their mortgage payments, and as they defaulted, houses started going up for sale. No buyers and too much supply. Lenders got stuck with bad loans and some of the big ones declared bankruptcy or were taken over. Big investors were hit hard and it wasn't only the banks embroiled in the mayhem.

Insurance companies couldn't save us

Investors had also bought over-the-counter derivatives and credit default swaps (CDOs). They were to serve as insurance against the mortgage-backed securities failing. AIG, a major US insurance company, sold billions of dollars-worth of CDOs without the cash to back them. On top of the CDOs, even more complex financial instruments got added to the mix. As AIG was considered 'too big to fail', the US Federal Reserve bailed out AIG to the tune of $182 billion (Amadeo, 2018).

Lehman Brothers

Lehman Brothers was the fourth largest investment bank in the USA. It had 25,000 employees worldwide. In 2003-2004 Lehmans acquired several mortgage lenders, making huge profits from sub-prime lending at first. In 2007 it had underwritten more mortgage-backed securities than any other company. This pre-empted its collapse, and on 15 September 2008 it filed for bankruptcy.

Frozen funds

Everything in the financial sector is connected. Large companies in the sector lacked a full grasp of their business. BNP Paribas was one of the top banks in the world with over 180,000 employees. In August 2007 it froze some of its funds. The bank was unable to value its sub-primed loan bundles or collateralized debt obligations (CDOs). They were too complex and likely unknowable (Bland, 2007).

Enter moral hazard. Where one person steps out into the road because they think someone else is looking out for traffic. Investors didn't guard against risk because they believed that credit agencies correctly rated financial products. Regulators failed to properly regulate the financial industry. They allowed it to regulate itself.

The bank bailout

The US government (the taxpayer) put up $700 billion to keep the banks liquid. Known as the bank bailout, the aim was to buy failed mortgage assets. Sharyl Attkisson reported on CBS News in 2009 (Attkisson, 2009) that the money enabled banks to buy other banks. Merrill Lynch received $10 billion while it was being bought up by Bank of America. Bank of America in turn received $15 billion bail-out money.

There is a bailout scorecard which shows where the money went and how it came back. AIG's figures ($67.8 billion) do not tally with the scorecard. The total provided in loans and purchased shares in the company was ($182 billion) (Nguyen, 2018).

A total of $631.9 billion went out:

Banks and Financial Institutions	$245 billion
Fannie and Freddie	$191 billion
Auto Companies	$79.7 billion
AIG	$67.8 billion
Mortgage Mod Program	$19.6 billion
Toxic Asset Purchases	$18.6 billion
State Housing Programs	$9.07 billion
Small Business Loan Aid	$368 million
FHA Refinance Program	£20 million

$728.5 billion came back:

Refunds – money returned to Treasury by bailed-out companies	$390 billion
Dividends – revenue Treasury has earned on its investments through dividends	$307 billion
Loan Interest	$1.83 billion
Selling Stock Warrants held on companies that paid back its investment	$9.63 billion
Revenue from fees and sales of equity or other Assets	$193.7 billion

The US government then went on to pass a stimulus package in January 2009. It pumped $800 billion into the economy through tax cuts and spending. In the UK, Royal Bank of Scotland received a £45.5 billion bailout from the government (taxpayers). This was to protect investors, businesses and personal clients relying on the bank. Recently RBS's chairman stated that the UK taxpayer will never recoup the full £45.5 billion invested (News, 2018).

The catastrophic failure of financial institutions led to regulatory reform. This included splitting the retail and investment arms of banks, ensuring that they had enough cash in reserve, in case something similar happened again. A few trillion bolting horses later, 8 million people in the US lost their jobs, 4 million lost their houses. In the UK we've only this year, 2019, 10 years later, come out of austerity (Mail, 2017). So, we paid the bailout with our taxes, and paid again with jobs, homes and stagnant pay. Very low interest rates force savers to invest more in precarious stock markets. Pension Funds in the US lost $2.5 trillion, and in the UK, the average pension is down by at least 15% (Sunderland, 2008).

Following the crisis, there was a massive sale of homes with sub-prime mortgages. The Blackstock Group is one of the largest investment companies in the world. It bought $5.5 billion single family homes to rent (Karmin, 2013). The Equities market is now the landlord of a new generation of American renters.

I do not pretend to understand the equities market, but there are 52,000 listed companies worldwide, and upwards of 3 million equity indexes (Reporting by Cezary Podkul. Produced by Gabriel Gianordoli, 2018). What exactly is it we're investing in you might ask?

The US treasury took on a lot of debt to backstop the financial system. As of August 2018, it owes $21.21 trillion (11%) US investors, the Federal Reserve and US government own $15 trillion (70.7%). Foreign investors own $6.21 trillion (29.3%). If another crisis emerged the authorities will have far less room for manoeuvre.

After 2008, trust in the financial sector is shaky. In 2011, Lord Turner, chair of the UK Financial Services Authority, issued a report on the failure of Royal Bank of Scotland. RBS purchased the Dutch Bank ABM Ambro in 2007, the eighth largest bank in

Europe. RBS didn't do proper due diligence. It wasn't looking (moral hazard lights blinking).

Lord Turner noted that another of the reasons the bank failed was 'underlying deficiencies in RBS management, governance and culture which made it prone to making poor decisions' (Bowers, 2011).

We trust institutions to be competent, accountable, honest and care for their customers. The RBS governors detached themselves from reality. They pursued power and wealth, overtaking Barclays Bank's bid for ABM Ambro to get there. They may have assumed Barclays had appraised the business so it was good to buy. Look for yourself when you're crossing the road or you could get hit by a massive Ambro.

Welcome to Bitcoin

In October 2008 an anonymous person or group of people, named Satoshi Nakamoto, released a Whitepaper. It proposed a person to person digital cash system called Bitcoin: no bank or third party necessary for people to send money to each other. In the introduction Satoshi stated that businesses need a lot of information about you, just so you can do a simple financial transaction. In turn you must trust that they will do right by you. Not only that but a certain amount of fraud in the banking world is accepted as unavoidable. If you use cash, you can avoid this. Bitcoin would be a decentralized electronic cash payment system, run on a blockchain, no blind trust involved (Nakamoto, 2008).

What is a Blockchain?

A blockchain is a shared public ledger. It is distributed across many computers, and, at first, lots of people volunteered their computer power to maintain it. Transactions involve people sending digital cash (Bitcoin) to one another. The blocks in the chain store information about the transactions, such as the date and time it was sent, the amount of Bitcoin sent and the signature (private key) of the owner. The chain is the public ledger which cryptographically links all the blocks.

Blockchain uses a two-key system, with a public and private key. The private key is used to sign transactions. Each block is unique and time-stamped, therefore it cannot be duplicated or reversed. Transactions are recorded publicly (so anyone can trace them back).

A revolution in transferring money from peer to peer. It was private, secure and trustless (you didn't have to trust a middle-man).

The unbanked and migrant workers: a use case for Bitcoin

Bitcoin would not just service people who had suffered from the stock market and bank failure in 2008. Two billion people in the world do not have bank accounts. They are unable to send money to each other.

Migrant workers sending money back to their families are hit with high bank fees. Often, they are sending only small amounts. A worker in the US sending money back to her family in Mexico might only send $50 at a time, but the bank fees incurred could be around $20. The banks are not geared to provide the best service for these types of clients. Bitcoin initially resolved the unbanked lack of access to making payments.

If people do not have a computer for online banking, many of them do have access to mobile phones. Bitcoin can be transferred via mobile Apps.

Bitcoin in development

Although the concept of sending cheap payments peer to peer is alive and well, Bitcoin technology needs to develop further to achieve its original goal. Another cryptocurrency, XRP, has already opened up extremely fast payment and settlement corridors. One of them is between the US and Mexico. Bitcoin can do the same but not as fast, and due to the current technology (as at January 2019), it's more expensive. Bitcoin developers are working on The Lightening Network. It will add another layer to the blockchain, speeding up transaction times.

Bitcoin is open source so developers continue to improve it. They fix bugs and add new functionality, as long as there is consensus in the network. If there isn't consensus it can, and has, resulted in hard forks. A hard fork is where there is divergence from the previous version of the blockchain and a split is created. In 2017 a group of Bitcoin developers, investors and miners wanted higher transaction speeds. Bitcoin could then be used as a faster transactional currency, rather than just a store of value, like gold and silver. They caused a split which resulted in Bitcoin Cash, a new coin.

Bitcoin as a store of value

Although people use Bitcoin to make payments, its other potential use is as a store of value, like gold and silver. Due to its mathematical properties it can't be counterfeited, and it is not heavy or hard to store, like gold. This secondary use was posited when the cost of sending Bitcoin became very expensive in 2017. This was due to a scaling issue, where the system could not handle the number of new users wanting to use Bitcoin.

How many Bitcoin are there?

The fact that there is a limited supply of Bitcoin means it can be considered as a store of value. There will be a maximum of 21 million Bitcoins, of which 17 million have been mined so far (April 2018). Each Bitcoin is divisible into a hundred millionths of a Bitcoin. These tiny fractions are called Satoshis.

Bitcoin opened up an opportunity to put *all* transactions on a blockchain, not just financial ones. There will be cryptocurrencies that can be programmed to represent assets. They could represent a vote in an election, or a land title. Grocers could show where the food in their shops was sourced from, showing a full history for all to see.

Bitcoin was hailed as an IT revolution, disruptive and reforming. Steve Wozniak, co-founder of Apple, compared fiat, gold and cryptocurrencies in a May 2018 article. He stated 'Gold gets mined and mined and mined. Maybe there's a finite amount of gold in the world, but cryptocurrency is even more mathematical and regulated and nobody can change mathematics' (Cuthbertson, 2018).

The cost of Bitcoin and Proof of Work

Bitcoin is mined, and it costs money to mine it. Bitcoin uses a Proof of Work algorithm to create its digital currency (an algorithm is a problem worked out by a computer). Miners compete against each other, working out complex maths puzzles using their computer power. When the puzzle is worked out the transactions are completed and the miners are given Bitcoin. The algorithm confirms transactions to produce new blocks on the chain.

Mining Bitcoin started as a cottage industry. It has become a large, specialised, industrial undertaking, using vast amounts of electricity. Bitcoin mining uses around 1% of the world's electricity. About the same as New York state's consumption, according to Arvind Narayanan, Associate Professor of Computer Science at Princetown University (Narayanan, 2018).

The cost of mining Bitcoin relies on the cost of electricity depending on which country you live in. As of May 2018, The Elite Fixtures Report revealed the cost of mining one Bitcoin in 115 countries. Venezuela is the cheapest at $531 per Bitcoin, and South Korea the most expensive at $26,170. In China, where a large proportion of Bitcoin is mined, it is estimated to cost $3,172 (Hankin, 2018).

Coinshares, an exchange traded platform, researched electricity consumption. They said 'It is…our belief that the claims around the environmental damage caused by cryptocurrency mining fundamentally miss out on the fact that many miners, in their self-serving search for the most cost-efficient form of electricity, have zoomed in on global regions with a glut of renewable electricity as prime locations for mining.' (Christopher Bendiksen, 2018).

22.4% of Bitcoin mining involves fossil/nuclear fuels. 77.6% uses renewable forms of energy, according to the Coinshares research. Crypto Bobby on Youtube explains the research in his video *Bitcoin mining in trouble? Examining the research and FUD* (3 December 2018). He suggests that the costs are overstated as there are many variables involved.

China mines approximately 75% of Bitcoin. As long as the retail price of Bitcoin is well above the cost price, it will be worthwhile mining it. Over the last year Bitcoin has gone down in value against the dollar. From a speculative high in December 2017 of $19,783 to its price today $3891 (3 January 2019).

51% Attacks on decentralized Bitcoin

Jihan Wu is the co-founder and CEO of Bitmain, which mines almost half of the world's Bitcoins. If one company owns 51% of the computing power (hash rate), then it is possible for them to change previous transactions. This would destroy the decentralised, trustless nature of the network. In 2014 GHash.io went over 51% control of hash rate, and took steps itself to reduce back down to 39% (Marinoff, 2018). Satoshi in his Whitepaper states, 'The system is secure as long as honest nodes collectively control more CPU power than any cooperating group of attacker nodes.'

Youtuber Ivan on Tech explains how a 51% attack could happen, in his video *Do you REALLY understand Bitcoin 51% Attack? Programmer explains.* Owning so much mining power could cause a monopoly, forcing other miners out of business, as they couldn't compete with the speed of the greater computing power. It would not be beneficial for any one entity to pursue a monopoly of Bitcoin mining though. It would become untrustworthy and worthless, Ivan states. A government takeover is a different matter. A government may want to destroy Bitcoin if it becomes too powerful. However, it would be difficult to take ownership of all the mining in that country. Miners could move their operations elsewhere. There is a bit of concern with so much mining concentrated in China, or any single country, for that matter.

Alt coins – new opportunities

Alt coins are the coins that came after Bitcoin, known as 'alternative' to Bitcoin. As of January 2019, there are 2102 alt coins in existence. Some of them improve on the original Bitcoin technology, by improving scalability (very important for millions of people using the software at the same time). Others have fewer or larger coin distributions, and are pre-mined (avoiding the big spend on electricity, and achieving a different purpose to Bitcoin). Some alt coins offer more privacy than Bitcoin. There are coins that offer nothing of great value and a whole bunch of them will likely fail in the future. However, many will be useful and change the way we live our lives. It's worth remembering that most crypto projects are still at the development stage.

To buy alt coins, up until recently, you would have to buy Bitcoin first with fiat currency (i.e. the currency associated with the country you live in, the dollar in the US or Yen in Japan). Cryptocurrency exchanges used Bitcoin to pair up with alt coins. On a weekly basis new exchanges and pairings are being created. You can buy XRP, Ethereum, Litecoin, Bitcoin Cash and others with fiat currency now. In some cases, you can buy other alt coins with Ethereum or XRP themselves.

Top ranking coins

In April 2013 the top five ranked cryptocurrencies (in order of market capitalization) (Coinmarketcap, 2013) were:

> Bitcoin ($1.5 billion);
> Litecoin ($74.4 million);
> Peercoin ($7.3 million);
> Namecoin ($6.4 million);
> Terracoin (1.5 million).

On 3 January 2019, those same coins look quite different:

Bitcoin remains number one ($67.84 billion);

Litecoin ranked 7 ($1.94 billion);

Peercoin ranked 160 ($16.69 million);

Namecoin ranked 229 ($10 million);

Terracoin ranked 915 ($486 thousand)

As at 3 January 2019 the top-ranking coins are totally different:

Ethereum (with a market capitalization of $15.67 billion);

XRP ($14.9 billion);

Bitcoin Cash ($2.89 billion);

EOS ($2.5 billion);

Stella ($2.21 billion).

Below rank three it's a bit of a moveable feast, but XRP and Ethereum have remained at the top for years.

XRP and Proof of Consensus

One of the leading Alt coins is XRP. XRP has been pre-mined, unlike Bitcoin which requires mining (proof of work). There are 100 billion XRP, because XRP is a coin to be used in the trillion-dollar banking and financial sectors. It is being used as a bridging currency to settle cross-border payments in real time. Using the XRP route, someone sending money to Mexico from the US will send US dollars – XRP – Mexican Pesos in seconds. They will use Ripple or R3 technology embedded into the banking software. The transaction is transparent, secure, low cost and immediate.

Established in 2012, XRP uses proof of consensus. David Schwartz is the Chief Technology Officer of Ripple. He describes consensus in his Youtube video, *Ripple and XRP – Part 7: Consensus vs. Proof of Work (2018)*. It uses a distributed ledger of nodes. No single node or person decides the outcome of a transaction on their own. Independent, trusted nodes in the network validate transactions in correct order. This avoids the double spend problem, where the same payment is made twice by mistake or fraudulently. The first transaction to be received is the one the nodes validate, and the second one is rejected. In her article on Ripple's website, *XRP Ledger Decentralizes Further with Expansion to 55 Validator Nodes*, Sarah Marquer writes 'While Bitcoin chooses validators solely on mining power, XRP Ledger validators are chosen based on performance, reliability, and security' (Marquer, 2019).

Ripple/R3 & XRP

Ripple is a company closely associated with XRP. At one time XRP and Ripple were considered the same thing, but they are not. At first Ripple owned most of the nodes, and it was considered to have a monopoly. Decentralization has been achieved by validator nodes being spread far and wide. These are some of the validators:

> Microsoft
>
> Massachusetts Institute of Technology (MIT)
>
> Telindus-Proximus Group (a telecommunications group)
>
> Worldlink (a global technology company)
>
> Bahnhof (one of Sweden's largest Internet providers)
>
> AT TOKYO Corporation (a data centre)
>
> CGI (a Canadian global IT consulting firm)
>
> Bitgo (a blockchain security company)

More companies and individuals are now validators. You can look at the Validator Registry here: https://xrpcharts.ripple.com/#/validators.
As of August 2018, Ripple runs only 10 of the 150 validators currently verifying transactions (Marquer, 2017).

Another company called R3 will also support XRP on its own platform (called Corda Settler). XRP is not solely connected to Ripple.

Some of R3s' partners include:

Amazon Web Services	Accenture
Barclays	BBVA
Citibank	Deutsche Bank
Hewlett Packard Enterprise	HSBC
HUAWEI	ING
Intel	Microsoft
MUFG	UBS

Ripple's customers include:

Santander	MUFG Bank
American Express	Yes Bank
Credit Agricole	Lian Lian Pay
Standard Chartered	SBI Remit

Moneygram, and hundreds more payment providers.

Both Ripple and R3 provide platforms which allow real-time cross-border payment and settlement. As XRP acts like a bridging currency, there is no need for clearing banks or Nostro and Vostro accounts. These accounts hold large stagnant pools of money on behalf of banks, so that their customers can send money abroad. If banks brought back these stagnant pools of money, they could profit more from re-investment. In turn the bank could offer customers better mortgage deals as they have more liquidity.

Ripple has connections to over forty of the world's central banks. These include the Bank of England, the US Federal Reserve, the Central Banks of New Zealand and Australia, the Saudi Arabian Monetary Authority, the Dutch Central Bank.

Ripple has many significant partnerships and production contracts with banks and money transfer companies all over the world. SBI Holdings (a financial services group in Japan) partnered with Ripple to form SBI Ripple Asia. In 2016 they formed a consortium of 61 Japanese banks, and in 2018 launched MoneyTap. This is a mobile phone app which uses Ripple's xCurrent technology to send domestic payments within Japan (Young, 2018). Youtuber Alex Cobb explains how MoneyTap could send cross-border payments using XRP to South Korea and Thailand in the near future (Cobb, 2018). xCurrent has recently integrated with xRapid, which uses the cryptocurrency XRP. If that is the most efficient way to send money, banks using the xCurrent software will be able to use XRP for instantaneous settlement (Walters, 2018). It will take a few seconds, with end-to-end tracking! It's dirt cheap to send, so institutions using XRP can send large amounts of money for peanuts.

Santander/American Express

Santander released their One Pay FX service using Ripple's xCurrent in April 2018. It is available to retail customers in the UK, Spain, Brazil and Poland (VK, 2018). Santander will soon increase the number of countries around the world that can access One Pay FX.

American Express will also use Ripple's blockchain for business customers. Payments are made between the UK and US on its FX International Payments (FXIP) (American Express, 2017).

SWIFT/XRP

Ripple technology is aimed at the banking sector, and competes with SWIFT. 11,000 financial institutions across 200 countries currently use SWIFT (Society for Worldwide Interbank Financial Telecommunication). It provides a secure messaging service between financial institutions, replacing the unsecure Telex messaging service of 45 years ago. SWIFT doesn't actually send the money across borders. It sends payment orders between intermediary banks in different counties. These intermediary banks take a fee at each stop, and transfers can take up to five working days. If they travel through countries with different currencies, banks can apply a bad exchange rate and keep the difference.

SWIFT, aware of disruptive competition from Ripple, have developed GPI (Global Payments Innovation) technology. It offers faster transactions, more transparent fees and end-to-end payment tracking than before. SWIFT GPI still remains a messaging system, based on an old infrastructure. XRP technology is very advanced in comparison. A third party distributed ledger technology like xRapid could potentially/hopefully be plugged into SWIFT's new system in the future (Mathew, 2018).

Ripple the company

Bitcoin has an invisible head, Satoshi Nakamoto. XRP has a major company, Ripple, promoting its use. Brad Garlinghouse, the CEO, promotes XRP around the world. The Chief Technology Officer David Schwartz is the co-creator of XRP and is a highly respected cryptographer. One of Ripple's founders, Chris Larsen co-founded mortgage lender e-loan, and the peer-to-peer lending platform Prosper Marketplace. He is pro consumer and advocated for the financial privacy of Californians, putting up $1million of his own money to stop financial service companies from selling people's personal information (Said, 2003).

Bitcoin, much like the Internet when it was first used, was associated with negative news and used for some nefarious activities. Bitcoin has moved on from these associations, but Ripple is actively promoting the crypto space in a positive way.

Ripple joined up with the Bill and Melinda Gates Foundation to set up Mojaloop (http://mojaloop.io/), for the two billion people across the world who don't have bank accounts. The Mojaloop software will bridge the gap between financial providers and mobile networks. Unlike the past associations of cryptocurrency with crime and the dark web, Ripple has improved the perception of crypto. The company donated $29 million to DonorsChoose.org, funding every single request for school materials made by American teachers in 2018. Ripple's PR tends towards donations to good causes.

XRP the standard

Compared to Bitcoin and Ethereum, XRP is currently faster and more scalable. Whereas XRP handles 1500 transactions per second, Ethereum does 15, and Bitcoin 3-6 (O'Keeffe, 2018). It's also faster. XRP settles payments in 4 seconds, Ethereum 2 or more minutes, Bitcoin over an hour. XRP is aiming to settle in 1 second.

Ethereum/Dapps/smart contracts

Another top cryptocurrency, in order of market cap is Ethereum, created by Vitalik Buterin. Ethereum is considered to be Bitcoin 2.0, the next level on. Bitcoin is a medium of payment and Ethereum is an open software platform for developers to build dApps and DAOs. dApps are decentralized applications on the secure blockchain and DAOs are decentralized autonomous organisations. Peer to peer contracts are made on the dApps. Where Bitcoin revolutionized payments, Ethereum will do the same on contracts.

Ether is the cryptocurrency that fuels the Ethereum network. Ethereum enables dApp creators to build on top of the Ethereum platform. They pay for each computational step they make using Ether. Producers get paid in Ether by the users of their smart contracts.

A dApp provides the infrastructure for several smart contracts. Smart contracts are small pieces of code executed on the block-chain. These contracts are agreements between two or more people/organisations, like any contract. They enable the fulfil-ment and enforcement of an agreed transaction. This reduces the costs of using a third party, like a bank, lawyer or estate agent.

Decentralisation on the Ethereum blockchain keeps large sensi-tive transactions safe. Personal data kept in an office can be breached by employees or hackers. Buying a house, for exam-ple, would be more secure on the blockchain within a smart contract.

Nick Szabo, a computer scientist first came up with the idea of smart contracts in 1993 (Szabo, 1994). Only when Bitcoin was conceived did it become possible to put Szabo's idea into action.

The possibilities of smart contracts are endless. Guarding your digital identity, for example by keeping all the information about yourself in one secure place on the blockchain. A place you can privately access and select which bits of information you would like to release, to get a loan, buy a house, get a job or some buy insurance. Another example would be simplifying the process of buying a flat by using legal agreements completed on the blockchain. OpenLaw, a blockchain-based system, teamed up with Ethereum, to improve the efficiency of buying and selling a property. Aaron Wright's Youtube video *Open Law – The End-to-End Purchase and Sale of Real Property* demonstrates how the smart contract is built.

Recording property ownership on the blockchain would make peoples' rights indisputable. Particularly useful in countries which don't have verified land titles.

Other use cases will be possible in the future, such as improving supply chains, maintaining tax records, transparent voting, and guarding intellectual rights (Ambisafe, n.d.).

Ethereum scaling up

Complex smart contracts will take some time to come to fruition, with the current slow transaction speeds. Ethereum is addressing scalability. Casper and Constantinople are upgrades that will change Ethereum from a proof of work to a proof of stake algorithm (Young, 2018). No easy thing. Constantinople is expected to go live in 2019 and other scaling elements in 2020 and 2021 (Kramer, 2018). Youtuber The Modern Investor discusses the Raidon Network Red Eyes in his video *Ethereum Raidon Network "Alpha" is live – 1 million Transactions per second* (The Modern Investor, 2018). It is currently being tested on the main network.

The Scalability Trilemma

What Bitcoin and Alt coins need to solve is known as the Scalability Trilemma. Steven Buchko describes the three features in his article Ethereum vs EOS (Buchko, 2018).

1. **Decentralization** permits censorship-resistance and enables anyone to take part in the system

2. **Security** means that the ledger cannot be changed, and the blockchain is able to resist 51% attacks

3. **Scalability** relates to the amount of transactions per second that can be processed on the network

As they exist now, Ethereum and Bitcoin prioritize decentralization and security. They are both working to improve scalability. The difficulty in achieving all three properties will take time.

There is a lot to be excited about in the crypto world. It's going to take time to achieve usable, scaled products. XRP has a completed product in use, but the task of Ripple and its partners is to sign up clients to use XRP. It has over 200 clients so far.

Ethereum ICOs/start-ups and current projects

Many new blockchain start-ups are being built on Ethereum. They raised money through ICOs (Initial Coin Offerings). In April 2017, 76% of new digital assets were built using the Ethereum network (Rowley, 2017). (Note that sometimes cryptocurrencies are called digital assets). There are believed to be 200,000 developers working on Ethereum smart contract expansion (Trustnodes, 2018).

As listed in the article by Daniel Frumpkin (Frumkin, 2018), some of the top 20 Etheruem projects are:

Binance Coin, BNB, for use to pay fees on Binance (the largest crypto exchanges in the world).

Maker, MKR, a stable coin.

OmiseGo, OMG, is developing Plasma, which will help scale up Ethereum. It is also aiming to offer the unbanked fast, secure payments.

0x, ZRX, a decentralized exchange network with smart contracts.

Basic Attention Token, BAT uses the Brave browser. It hands back control to advertisers and content publishers. BAT cuts out the Facebooks and Youtube middlemen.

Pundi X, NPXS, a point of sale device for merchants to use crypto-currencies in shops.

Chainlink, LINK, allows smart contracts secure access to external data.

Populous, PPT is a peer-to-peer system. It gives loans to businesses based on their future earnings.

TrueUSD, TUSD, a stable coin.

Golem, GNT, is a decentralized supercomputer. Combining the unused power of people's computers around the world. It provides a resource for complex computations and tasks. Tasks such as AI development or medical research.

Decentraland, MANA, is a virtual reality platform. You can buy plots of land which you can then build anything you want on.

Ethereum smart contract competitors

Ethereum has its competitors, which are also building smart contracts. Some are listed below:

EOS (decentralized applications platform);

NEO (distributed smart economy network);

Cardano (a smart contract platform);

TRON (decentralized entertainment content sharing platform);

Lisk (decentralized applications);

Codius (smart contracts platform).

EOS – an Ethereum competitor

EOS was co-founded by Brock Pierce, Brendan Blumer and Dan Larimer in 2017. After a year-long Initial Coin Offering, ending in May 2018, EOS raised $4 billion in investment. They created a decentralized application platform which processes 6000 transactions per second. Those transactions are free, which is valuable to new developers.

Youtuber Cypherglass describes the benefits of not paying fees on the EOS platform compared to Ethereum's current model in his video *Usability on the EOS Network*. He compares paying a fee for everything you did on Facebook, like 'liking' a post. That's the current Ethereum model, where you have to pay a fee for every transaction (Cypherglass, 2018).

Cypherglass also explains that EOS is more user friendly than other platforms, with readable usernames and password/account recovery. Ethereum uses long, impossible to remember account names. If you send money to the wrong account name, your money is irretrievable. On EOS you have three days to get it back.

Andrew Macdonald compares Ethereum to EOS in his article *EOS vs Ethereum: Predicting the Winner of the Smart Contract War*. He is concerned that Ethereum doesn't let its developers build consumer-grade applications. These are applications that need no training by consumers to use them. He writes 'Ethereum's main use case is supposed to be supporting applications, but less than 10% of the total transactions on the network are coming from the top 100 applications built on Ethereum. The other 90% of transactions are coming from ICOs and payments. The next few months will be a pivotal point for smart contracting platforms, and specifically Ethereum, because major applications such as Augur, Golem, and Mana (Decentraland) are launching on their platform, and if Ethereum cannot support the transaction throughput for these applications, which have combined valuations greater than $1.2B USD, they will be forced to build on top of a more scalable platform' (Macdonald, 2018).

EOS, he maintains *is* building consumer-grade applications. Everipedia (a blockchain encyclopedia) is one example.

EOS – Delegated Proof of Stake

EOS employs Delegated Proof of Stake (DPoS). Twenty-one block producers are voted in to keep the network secure and validate transactions. DPoS enables EOS to run faster than Ethereum currently does. However, there are concerns over centralization, with a such small group of validators (Lielacher, 2018). One EOS token equals one vote, therefore if somebody owns and stakes a million EOS, they have a million votes. Starteos, a Chinese blockchain company is one of the 21 block producers running the network. They have recently declared that they will buy votes from EOS block voters. Youtuber Crypto Tim takes them to task on his video *Crypto Tim's candid response to Starteos* (CyptoTim, 2018). One of the co-founders takes a different view. Brendan Blumer tweeted on 1 January 2019 'The #EOS community should consider the introduction of voter rebates from BP candidates to introduce free market pricing to block production, drive more value back to token holders, and increase voter turnout. Unenforceable rules only hurt the compliant' (BrendanBlumer, 2019). Brendan wants to encourage voting by all stakeholders. Paying them to vote would be an incentive and EOS investors would benefit from holding their coins and participating more. Voting on EOS will be revised soon with the consensus of the stakeholders.

EOS – digital real estate

Like all blockchain technologies EOS is a work in progress. One with immense possibilities. Youtuber The Awakenment describes EOS as digital real estate in an illuminating video. He tells us there will be a total of 1 billion EOS tokens, but not all of them will be staked on the EOS platform. Some of them will remain unregistered. Some EOS tokens will be left on exchanges. Only staked tokens on the EOS network will be used to rent out CPU and RAM to dApp producers.

As of December 2018, 48% of EOS tokens are staked. Block-one, the originators of EOS will retain 10% of the space. As a stake holder, he posits, you own the virtual office space in which creators make dApps. They rent your staked tokens. Some dApp producers themselves will also buy floor space (staked tokens) and keep hold of them. The more successful a dApp becomes, the more space it will need. They will have to buy more EOS or rent it from existing stakeholders, making EOS tokens scarce and more valuable (The Awakenment, 2017). The video is called *EOS = Blockchain Real Estate. How the price of EOS tokens will increase over time*, and he follows it up with an update *How EOS is creating its own Economy + Update to Blockchain Real Estate* (The Awakenment, 2018).

It's possible to earn interest if you hold EOS. Youtuber EOS Tips demonstrates how to earn interest with your EOS tokens by staking and lending them using Chintai (a token leasing platform) via a Scatter wallet. His video is called *How to earn interest on your EOS tokens using Chintai* (EOS Tips, 2018). Note that there is a difficulty factor in setting up accounts and wallets for EOS. It is worth it in the end, and there are Youtube videos showing you how.

If you stake your tokens on the EOS platform, you cannot sell them on an exchange until you un-stake them. It takes three days to un-stake them.

EOS Airdrops

The good thing about staking your EOS token is that you receive airdrops. These are coins from new start-ups that are deposited for free in your EOS wallet. You receive coins proportional to the amount of staked EOS in your wallet.

Why would they give you coins for free? It's a way of making you aware of their project, instead of paying to advertise it. The start-up may airdrop 30% of their tokens, keeping the remaining 70% for themselves. As more people get to know about the project and use it, the value of the coin rises. The owners can raise investment on the tokens they still hold.

On the Ethereum model new start-ups raised money by issuing millions of ERC20 tokens and sold them to keen investors. (ERC-20 tokens are a standard coin issued on the Ethereum platform. It means start-ups don't have to invent their own coin technology from scratch). The start-ups that go on to build a functional product will gain in value, and the original investors can make a lot of money. However, there were quite a few that stopped developing their projects and skipped town with the investors' cash. Some will genuinely have been unable to keep financing the development of their projects.

How to size up a cryptocurrency

Different types of cryptocurrency

There are different types of cryptocurrency. With over 2,000 cryptocurrencies out there you need a bit of help navigating your way around. Cryptomaniacs.com is a very useful website to help you learn, with information and short videos on over 70 of the top coins. Below is a list of five types:

Currency coins, for monetary exchange:

Bitcoin	XRP	Litecoin	Stella
Bitcoin Cash	Bitcoin SV	DASH, Maker	Dogecoin
Decred	Nano	Digibyte	Komodo
Electroneum	Bitcoin Diamond		

Privacy coins are untraceable:

Monero	Zcash	Bytecoin	Pivx

Decentralized Apps (dApps):

Ethereum	EOS, Cardano	TRON	Nem
Etherium Classic	NEO	Ontology	Waves
Qtum	Lisk	Zilliqa	Siacoin
Basic Attention Token		Stratis	Aeternity
Augur	Steem	Factom	Glem
Status	Populous	Ark	Icon

Supply Chain Protocols make data transactions along the supply chain easier:

Iota	VeChain	Waltonchain

Cryptocurrency Exchanges are online platforms where you can trade in cryptocurrencies:

BinanceCoin	Omisego	0x
Bitshares	KuCoin	GXChain

Hard forks – you go your way and I go mine

Some coins are hard forks of other coins. A hard fork is a new version of the blockchain protocol, resulting in a complete split from the older version. People using the platform either have to use the new protocol or continue using the old one. They are now parallel source codes with new transaction histories. Bitcoin Cash, Bitcoin Gold, Bitcoin Private and Litecoin are all hard forks of Bitcoin.

In November 2018 Bitcoin Cash split further into Bitcoin ABC and Bitcoin SV. This was a publicly fraught split between two vocal proponents, Roger Ver and Craig Wright. Ver and Jihan Wu wanted to remove the limit on the block size of Bitcoin Cash to be able to support smart contracts. Craig Wright wanted to retain the vision of Satoshi Nakamoto. He maintained Bitcoin Cash should only be used as a peer to peer money transfer coin (Huang, 2018). Despite the mathematics of the blockchain, our human frailties can't help but get in the way! Roger Ver showed the world Wright's email prior to the split, which started 'If you want a war…I will do 2 years of no trade. Nothing. In the war, no coin can trade…' (Ver, 2018). Craig threatened to sell a huge amount of Bitcoin in order to crash the market. It caused uncertainty in the cryptocurrency market, and coins sank further in price than expected (Cant, 2018).

What does a cryptocurrency do and who is behind it?

Once you work out what a particular coin does, ask what problem does it solve. Investinblockchain.com provides a helpful list of the top 100 coins describing what they do in ten words (Bardinelli, 2018). You can also read the Whitepaper associated with a project. However, Whitepapers can be like marketing tools, so do independent research on Cryptos that interest you.

Review information on the associated website. Who is behind the project, who are the team and what is their business background? Do they have a social media presence and how versed are they in blockchain technology? Are they adequately funded? Do they have a roadmap, and have they achieved the goals they've set themselves?

Brendan Eich created Java Script. He is the founder of BAT (Basic Attention Token). BAT is a decentralized advertising exchange associated with the Brave browser. Brian Bondy is the co-founder of BAT, and he worked on Firefox and the Khan Academy. They raised $2.5 million from angel investors for BAT. The website's About Us page displays a large group of software engineers and researchers (https://brave.com/about/). The Brave browser already works, so it can be used right now. A team with so much previous experience and expertise gives you more confidence in a project.

Dan Larimer of EOS has already created two blockchain platforms, Steemit and Bitshares. EOS has an enormous financial war chest to develop the network, $4 billion. You can probably expect great things from EOS.

Does the project already have an active following? Kin coin is associated with Kik, a mobile chat app for teenagers. Kin tokens can be earned to spend on premium themes on the Kik app. Kik, as of 2016 has over 300 million registered users, with over 9 million active users monthly (Statista, 2018).

Gaming

What industries are coins associated with? The gaming industry is worth over $100 billion. It might be worth looking at coins developing for that market. Some examples of gaming coins are:

Enjin Coin (ENJ)	Chimaera (CHI)
Ethbet (EBET)	Decentraland (Mana)
RevolutionVR (RVR)	MobileGo (MGO)
GameCredits (GAME)	FirstBlood (1ST)

Coin price

What about the price of a coin? Bitcoin is currently trading around $4,000. Should you buy it instead of XRP, which is trading at around 40 cents. If you buy $100 worth of XRP you will receive 250 XRP. If you buy $100 worth of Bitcoin you will receive 0.025 of a Bitcoin. It looks like you would be better off buying XRP because you would have more of them, but how many you own does not matter. What is important is the percentage increase in a coin over time. Also, you don't have to buy a whole coin – you can buy a fraction of a Bitcoin. Coinmarketcap.com will give you current prices, volume and market capitalization on all cryptocurrencies.

Working products – can I use it yet?

Which projects already have working products? Despite their relative lack of speed and scalability, Bitcoin and Ethereum do have platforms that are being used. XRP has a fully working software product. However, as noted before, all these products are in their infancy. The products associated with XRP need time to be integrated in banking and other financial institutions' software. Bitcoin and Ethereum need to scale their technology.

Other products that you can actually use right now are:

Bitcoin Cash	Litecoin	Stella	Monero-
NEO	Binance Coin	Zcash	Qtum
0x	Bytecoin	Decred	Bitshares
Steem	Siacoin	Auger	Nano
Basic Attention Coin		Golem	Pundi X
Waves	KuCoin	Wanchain	Komodo
Ardor	Huobi	Zencash	Pivx
Kyber	Bancor	Tether	Loom
Polymat	Bibox	Dash	

Invest in Blockchain provide the above list with descriptions for each one (Invest in blockchain, 2018).

Cryptos in the top 15 with no working product as yet: TRON, Cardano and IOTA.

How to buy cryptocurrency

Make a plan

Once you have settled on a coin that you like, make a plan. Financial advisors often tell people to diversify, so you could choose three to five coins (any more than five makes it difficult to keep up with). If you don't feel confident in choosing more than one coin at first, because there is a lot to learn, don't worry, stick with what you know. I am not a financial advisor so you will have to make your own decisions about what you do.

Be clear about how much you want to invest. Imagine yourself going to Las Vegas, knowing you're likely to lose your money but have a good time trying to win. Crypto markets are very volatile, and at this point in time few people have got a handle on them. Better regulation is ahead, but it's not here yet.

Be conscious of the emotional factor. You feel good if the market goes up, but if you are unsure about the coin you've bought, and it goes down suddenly, it's possible you will be fearful and sell at the wrong price.

Invest in what you understand. Decide what price you want to sell at. Exchanges will allow you to put up sell orders at higher prices. If it reaches that price your coins will be sold, even if you are asleep or on holiday. You can also put up buy orders at the price you would like to buy. Remember crypto markets are open every minute of the day, every day of the year. When you go to bed in South Korea, investors are waking up in the US. When markets go up dramatically it is as stressful as when they go down. Have a plan that takes all the emotion out of your decision-making. Keep track of what price you bought the coin. You might buy the same coin at different prices on different days.

Some Youtubers offer technical analysis (TA), but even TA can trap you into believing you know what is going to happen in the crypto market. Whatever you end up doing, you, like everyone else, will learn the hard way. So have a plan.

Trading on exchanges

The way to profit using crypto, is exchanging your fiat currency (i.e. the currency belonging the country you live in, like the UK Pound, US Dollar, Russian Ruble, Euro, South Korean Won, South African Rand) in the hope that the cryptocurrency rises against the fiat currency.

A cryptocurrency exchange is a website or mobile phone app where you can buy, sell and exchange cryptocurrencies. More and more exchanges are opening. Many allow you to buy crypto with fiat.

To open an account on good exchanges, you will need to set up an account and provide identification. On Bancour exchange I had to send a video of myself holding up my driving licence, while saying that I understood what Bitcoin was! That was the most work I've done to open an account. I did it because Bancor lists EOS airdropped tokens, which few other exchanges do.

There are plenty of Youtube videos showing you, step by step, how to open an account on a particular exchange. They will also demonstrate how to deposit funds, and then exchange those funds for cryptocurrency.

Coinbase is the biggest US exchange, and it can be used by people living in the UK, US, Europe, Australia, Canada and Singapore. You can deposit money with your debit or credit card, and in some cases send money from your bank account.

Bitstamp lets you deposit money by bank transfer and credit card.

Gatehub has the cheapest XRP prices. You can send a bank transfer which will turn into Euros or US dollars, and then you exchange them for XRP, Bitcoin, Ethereum, DASH, Ethereum Classic, and Bitcoin Cash.

The London Block Exchange is for UK investors. You need to make a bank transfer.

Binance is the biggest crypto exchange in the world. It lists hundreds of coins.You can send Euros and UK pounds to buy cryptocurrency, but not other fiat currencies as yet. For other countries you must buy Ethereum, XRP or Bitcoin on another exchange and then transfer the coin you bought to Binance. The benefit of Binance is that it lists coins that other exchanges have not listed yet.

Binance is highly thought of in the crypto space.

Exchanges are pairing the top coins such as Bitcoin, Ethereum and XRP with newer coins. There was a time when you could only buy other coins with Bitcoin. There is now more liquidity between cryptocurrencies.

If you do send cryptocurrency between exchanges do a test run first, sending the minimum allowed, and make sure it arrives at its destination before sending more.

I would stay well away from margin trading, where you borrow money from the exchange to buy crypto. If things go wrong, you will lose the money you put in and the money you borrowed. **Investing in cryptocurrency is a high-risk venture. Only invest what you can afford to lose.**

The exchanges I've used and recommend are:

Binance	Bitstamp	Bancor	Gatehub

Well known exchanges, not listed above:

Uphold	Bittrex	OKEx	Kraken
Huobi	Gemini	Coinsquare	Bithumb
SBI Virtual Currencies		Poloniex	Kucoin
Coins.ph	Cryptopia	Coinone	Bitrue
Korbit	Upbit	Coinbase	Modiax
Bitfinex	Changegelly	CEX.io	Coinfield
Biccos	Bitso		

Security/keeping your crypto safe

Cryptocurrencies are different to fiat currencies. You can't put them in a bank account, you have to look after them yourselves. If you trade on a daily basis, keeping your crypto on an exchange is useful. If anything happened to the exchange, like a hack, you could possibly lose your crypto. The coins are not in your custody, they belong to the exchange. It is therefore safer to own a crypto wallet.

A wallet has a pair of very long alpha-numeric keys – a private and a public key. You must keep your keys secure. The private key is like a PIN, keep it secret. The public key is like a bank account number. If you want to transfer crypto to yourself, or have crypto sent to you from someone else, you need to let them have your public key. Do not give them your private key. Otherwise they can take your coins away from you.

There are different types of wallets. Alongside is a table showing the top wallets, taken from Suji Velu's, article *How to keep your cryptocurrency safe: 7 must have wallets* (Velu, 2018).

Keepkey, Nano Ledger S and Trezor are hardware wallets. These wallets are physical devices, a bit like a USB stick, that keep your private key safe. They keep your crypto offline, away from hackers.

Coinbase is a web-based exchange, and they keep your crypto offline, and insure it against loss. This appears to be the easiest method for new people, but Coinbase currently offers only a selection of cryptocurrencies. They will be expanding into new cryptocurrencies in the future, but they don't offer XRP yet, so you are better off with a Nano S in this case (I believe Uphold, which does list XRP will offer crypto insurance in the future). The Youtube video by Gary Cruz, *How to move Ripple to a Ledger Nano S from Binance* shows you how to set up a Ledger Nano S and send XRP from the Binance exchange. I realize that anyone new to crypto will see that last sentence as foreign. It will make sense once you explore crypto a bit more.

	Cost	Security	Mobility	User-friendliness	Convenience	Style
KeepKey	$99	Ported Trezor's code and firmware	Largest hardware wallet, requires USB	Simple UI	Requires USB and password authentication	Anodized aluminium OLED display
Nano Ledger S	$65	Use of a Secure Element[10]	Medium sized hardware wallet, requires USB	Simple UI	Requires USB and password authentication	Thumb drive shaped
Trezor	$99	Reputation for gold standard security in crypto wallet	Smallest hardware wallet, requires USB	Simple UI	Requires USB and password authentication	Shock tolerant design
Coinbase	Free	Multiple layers of security and 100% crypto insurance	Web-based	Beginner friendly	Instant and free transfer to GDAX, Buy and sell crypto online	Beginner friendly
MEW	Free	Offline GitHub download available	Private Keys are recorded down	Steep learning curve to achieve security	Requires authentication	
Jaxx	Free	New updates might not be fully stable	Available on all platforms and mobile devices	Shapeshift integration	Mobile interface	Pleasant App UI
Electrum	Free	Multi-sig	Predominan	Lightweight	Desktop	

As some exchanges charge more to trade or transfer cryptocurrencies, it is worth looking at their fees before subscribing. Using a Ledger Nano S to store your crypto means you can choose any exchange you prefer. The Nano S supports 700 cryptocurrencies. Ledger.com provides a list of all the digital assets it can store on its Supported Crypto Assets page (ledger.com, 2019).

My Ether Wallet (MEW) is useful to store Etheruem or any token built on its platform. MEW does not store your coins, it gives you an address for people to send you coins. You store the keys on your computer or a hardware wallet. It's free, a bit complicated to use, but important for Ethereum users.

Greymass and Scatter are desktop wallets for EOS. Scatter does a chrome extension wallet, but it is safer to use their desktop version. Greymass is a wallet you can use to vote for the 21 EOS block producers. You can also stake and un-stake your tokens. Both wallets can transfer EOS and EOS airdropped tokens from or to exchanges or other people.

Which countries support cryptocurrencies?

Bitcoin has no country. There is no coordinated, international regulation of cryptocurrencies. Each sovereign country applies its own rules. Many countries are waiting to see how things turn out elsewhere.

Australia & New Zealand

Australia's government is very positive towards Bitcoin. It views it like any other currency. New Zealand sees it as a payment system not a currency.

UK, USA, Canada, Europe

The USA, Europe and Canada are watching and assessing. Belgium and Finland regard Bitcoin as a commodity and give it VAT exempt status. In the USA and Israel Bitcoin is classed as a property, and therefore subject to property taxes. In the UK it is classed as currency. Profits made on exchanging cryptocurrency are liable for personal tax, corporation tax or capital gains tax. It depends on whether profits were made from day trading (personal or corporation tax) or long-term investment (capital gains tax) (HMRC, 2018).

The UK, USA and Canada want regulations to support cryptocurrencies. Many countries require cryptocurrency exchanges to obtain identification from customers. This is to counter money-laundering and other criminal activities. In the US, the Commodity Futures Trading Commission (CFTC) and the Securities and Exchange Commission (SEC) regulate cryptocurrencies. The CFTC appears to be more upbeat on crypto than the SEC. The SEC has refused a few applications for Bitcoin ETFs (Exchange Traded Funds) to date. The whole market is watching its next move (Maurya, 2018). February 2019 will see the SEC rule on the VanEck Bitcoin ETF, a well-considered application from the New York-based investment management company.

XRP is affected by bank compliance and regulation. Whilst it has worked hard to be compliant with financial institutions, Ripple is still working with regulators around the globe to move regulation forward. In fact, they have a team dedicated for this purpose alone.

Top crypto-friendly countries

The top 12 countries trying to attract cryptocurrency businesses and adopt Bitcoin are (Hay, 2018):

1. Malta	5. Slovenia	9. Belarus
2. Bermuda	6. Singapore	10. Hong Kong
3. Switzerland	7. Estonia	11. Japan
4. Gibraltar	8. Georgia	12. Germany

These countries offer favourable tax regimes relating to cryptocurrency. Thomson Reuters published a list of cryptocurrencies by country in 2017. In their Answers for Tax Professionals section, they outline each countries' take on digital assets (Thomson Reuters, 2017).

Japan

In 2014 Mt Gox, a Japanese cryptocurrency exchange, went bankrupt after it was hacked. 850,000 Bitcoins had been stolen over several years.

Japan changed its Payment Services Act in April 2017, legalizing digital currency. It also regulated the country's exchanges to safeguard their customers (Hamilton, 2018). However, in January 2018, an even bigger hack took place on Coincheck, another Japanese exchange. $534 million worth of NEM (the coin for a smart-assets platform), was stolen. Unlike Mt Gox, Coincheck did not leave its customers in the lurch and file for bankruptcy. Instead it found the account where the stolen NEM was being held. Coincheck promised to refund the coins to its customers. (Pollock, 2018). Japan remains positive despite these attacks. It has sixteen licensed exchanges, and 160 new operators would like to open exchanges in Japan (Helms, 2018).

Japan classifies cryptocurrencies as miscellaneous income. Crypto-currencies are taxed at a rate of between 15% and 55%, depending on how much people earn (Emem, 2018).

South Korea

In South Korea there are over 100 exchanges. The Korean government is moving to regulate them (Review, 2018).

Wealthy families in South Korea own large conglomerates (known as chaebols). Samsung, Hyundai, SK Group and LG are some examples (The Korea Herald/Asia News Network, 2016). The chaebols are backing new digital asset start-ups and exchanges and testing blockchain networks.

SK Telecom backs the cryptocurrency exchange Korbit, and Nexon (a huge gaming giant), is also backing Korbit. The second largest bank in the country Shinhan Bank set up Gopax, a new crypto exchange. The exchange is regulation-compliant. It can transfer funds instantaneously to the crypto exchange (Young, 2018). Anyone who has sent funds from a bank knows it can take three frustrating days to reach an exchange. Shinhan Bank and Woori Bank have both tested Ripple's software (Dixit, 2018). Both banks will integrate the software in 2019 (Young, 2018).

Thailand

While the US regulatory bodies ponder what to do with crypto-currencies, Thailand has swept ahead. Thailand is making its regulations and company licences straight forward. Exchanges and start-ups work with regulators as they set up their companies, so compliant frameworks are already established and approved. Thai regulators are truly engaged with the new technology They have met with experts like Vitalik Buterin (co-founder of Ethereum) and the Omisego team (Yang, 2018).

China

In China, the story is quite different. The Chinese government were concerned by 90% of Bitcoin trading occurring in China. They outlawed the purchase of Bitcoin with Renminbi (China's fiat currency) on exchanges. In response the big exchanges in China moved to other countries. Huobi moved to Singapore. OKex and Binance relocated to Malta (Canellis, 2018). You can own cryptocurrency and you can also spend it in China. How you get it I don't know, unless it's leftover Bitcoin before the exchanges left.

India

About 80% of Indians have bank accounts (Global Findex, 2017), and India receives the most remittances in the world. $65 billion received in 2017 (The World Bank, 2017). Digital currencies could work well in the country. Ripple recently set up an office in Mumbai, hoping to improve payment and settlement services for millions of people. Several Indian banks are interested in the xCurrent technology. Kotak Mahindra Bank and Axis Bank are two of them.

The government of India banned crypto in 2017. They changed their policy in 2018, and will legalize it with strong regulations (Shukla, 2018).

Chile, Bolivia, Ecuador

In South America, Chile is embracing cryptocurrency. It is also protecting its people by issuing regulation to stop money-laundering. Bolivia, on the other hand, banned Bitcoin. The government worries that it would destabilize the monetary system. In Ecuador Bitcoin can't be used to make payments within the country.

Argentina

Argentina's Central Bank pushed for cryptocurrency regulation. It hosted a G20 meeting this year, where cryptocurrency regulation was discussed. The country is a positive adopter of cryptocurrency.

Argentina suffered from an inflation rate of 20,000% in 1990. The Argentinian Peso is not in a good state, with inflation at around 30% today. People prefer US dollars instead, hiding them in the walls of their houses. In recent years, they have embraced cryptocurrency, more likely to use crypto wallets instead of cash stuffed in the walls. Four thousand Bitcoin ATMs (cash machines) will be installed in Argentina (Thomson, 2018). It makes you wonder whether a digital asset like Bitcoin, XRP or DASH could eventually replace a fiat currency.

Venezuela

Venezuela also suffered hyperinflation deflating the value of the Bolivar (Venezuela's fiat currency). The IMF (International Monetary Fund) predicts one million per cent inflation by the end of 2018! (Chandler, 2018). Bitcoin and DASH (a digital cash coin) are very popular in Venezuela. The government launched its own oil-backed cryptocurrency, the Petro, and is providing free courses in how to mine, buy and sell digital currencies.

Mexico

Mexico is keen to take advantage of the economic benefits crypto could bring to the country. The government recently passed regulations to make dealing in currencies more trustworthy (Malwa, 2018).

Ricardo Anaya was one of Mexico's recent presidential candidates. He proposed using the blockchain to keep the election transparent. He was fighting corruption in a country with more bribery than in any other country in Latin America (Lanz, 2018).

Brazil

Banks in Brazil are closing accounts related to crypto. Large fees and bureaucracy prevent 60 million people in Brazil from even having a bank account. Despite the hostile banking environment, businesses in Brazil are making progress in the use of digital assets. Fintech company Nubank launched a credit card digital app for mobile phones (Mari, 2017). There are 208 million people living in Brazil, and 198 million smart phones (Chang, 2017). Airfox, a mobile financial services company released a free app. People without bank accounts can now buy things using their smart phones.

They can also use their mobile devices to take out microloans, bypassing the banks completely (cointelegraph.com, 2018). CoinBR, a Brazilian cryptocurrency company, has partnered with DASH to offer digital cash in 13,000 locations (Buck, 2017). The Central Bank of Brazil partnered up with R3 in 2017 (Castillo, 2017) to use its Corda distributed ledger. Corda Settler (also known as Finextra) can use XRP for immediate payments and settlements (Huillet, 2018). This will surpass anything the banks can do.

Brazil's Real Estate Registry Office has partnered with US blockchain real estate company Ubituity LLC. They will keep unchangeable land ownership records on the blockchain, overcoming corruption and lack of good property record-keeping (Allison, 2017).

Zimbabwe, Ghana and Nigeria

Bitcoin has been adopted in Zimbabwe, Ghana and Nigeria due to high inflation rates.

Political instability in some African countries could make cryptocurrencies attractive. However, the price volatility may prove very risky. Crypto price volatility is universal in all countries in the world, for that matter.

In some African nations, lack of internet access and power supply may slow down the initial uptake of cryptocurrencies. (Rao, 2018)

Saudi Arabia, Bahrain, Kuwait, Cyprus, Israel

In the Middle East different nation states are at different stages of adoption and regulation. The Saudi Arabian Monetary Authority and the Bahrain Central Bank are forward-thinking. They are connecting positively with blockchain technologies. Other countries in the region are pursuing blockchain-powered projects through central governments. Qatar is looking at Ethereum. Saudi Arabia is also interested in Ethereum and XRP/Ripple. The Kuwait Finance House will also be using Ripple's software.

Ripple donated $50 million towards the University Blockchain Research Initiative. This is for universities around the world. The University of Nicosia in Cyprus is using the fund for a Master of Science Degree in Digital currency.

Israel will receive $100 million from Czech investment banking firm Benson Oak. The money will to go towards blockchain start-ups (O'Neal, 2018). Israel is keen to foster new crypto start-ups, striking a balance between regulation and growth (Bitcoin Exchange Guide News Team, 2018).

IMF and World Bank

The World Bank and International Monetary Fund are looking at blockchain and consensus technologies. They want to increase economic growth around the world. They hope that crypto can address bribery and endemic corruption. The blockchain offers immutability and transparency, giving people faith in recorded documentation. A good example is the technology company Bitfury Group. It is signing a deal with the government of Georgia to register land titles. This would change people's lives. They would gain an immutable document proving they own a parcel of land (Wellisz, 2018).

The big guns are here

Institutional investors, like banks, mutual funds or unit trusts, are gearing up to board the crypto train in 2019. The volatility in the crypto markets is attractive to investors, who may well see the potential for big returns. There has been a continuous bear market in 2018, and cryptos are at bargain prices. Over the counter (OTC) purchases of cryptos by hedge funds are occurring in private. These purchases are outside of the retail exchanges that you and I would use. Miners are selling direct to these clients starting at $100 thousand lump sum purchases.

Goldman Sachs / New York Stock Exchange

Goldman Sachs is offering a Bitcoin traded product. The owner of the New York Stock Exchange will soon provide a Bitcoin futures product, Bakkt. They have raised $182.5 million of investment. It will have actual warehoused Bitcoins backing it (Arnold, 2018). They are waiting for clarification from the Commodity Futures Trading Commission before launch. The launch has been postponed a couple of times.

Switzerland's Stock Exchange

Switzerland's Stock Exchange is launching a trading and custodial exchange (Six Group, 2018). Custodial management of crypto will make it possible for the big investors to come on board. In the same way that a bank holds your money in an account so you don't have to hide cash under the bed, custodial managers will warehouse your crypto securely. Individuals holding cryptos often leave them on an exchange. Some exchanges were hacked in the past and cryptos lost. Currently, crypto can be held in a computer/mobile phone wallet, a paper wallet or hardware wallet.

TD Ameritrade / Fidelity/ Nasdaq

TD Ameritrade, a brokerage company with $1.297 trillion in client assets, has invested in ErisX. ErisX is a digital exchange offering Bitcoin, Ethereum, Litecoin and Bitcoin Cash and probably XRP (Rooney, 2018).

Fidelity which holds $7.2 trillion in client assets, will provide a custodial trading service. Fidelity Digital Assets will offer Bitcoin and Ethereum and other unnamed cryptocurrencies (De, 2018).

The Nasdaq (stock exchange) are joining with VanEck (an investment management company). They will sell Bitcoin futures in the first quarter of 2019 (Rooney, 2018). VanEck are seeking a decision from the US Securities and Exchange Commission on their first Bitcoin exchange-traded fund.

Youtube sources

Youtube channels to watch for reliable, fact-based information, with some fun thrown in. Below are the ones I like to watch. They keep you going, through the bear markets, and grounded in the bull markets. A big thank you to all of them.

They also show you how to open Scatter or Greymass wallets, how to buy a Nano S or Trezor wallet to keep your crypto offline and safe.

Youtubers keep you up-to-date on Airdrops, Initial Coin Offerings, and recent developments in crypto.

Bitcoin and other crypto

Alessio Rastani
https://www.youtube.com/user/alessiorastani/videos

Altcoin Buzz
https://www.youtube.com/channel/UCGyqEtcGQQtXyUwvcy7Gmyg/videos

Boxming
https://www.youtube.com/channel/UCxODjeUwZHk3p-7TU-IsDOA/videos

Chris Dunn
https://www.youtube.com/channel/UCdC3h2m88FC02YwA_VESRQ

Colin Talks Crypto
https://www.youtube.com/channel/UCnqJ2HjWhm7MbhgFHLUENfQ/videos

Crypto Coin News
https://www.youtube.com/channel/UCkpt3vvZ0Y0wvTX2L-lkxsg/videos

Cryptocurrency Market
https://www.youtube.com/user/PrisonOrFreedom/videos

Crypto Investor
https://www.youtube.com/channel/UC93MJYEjwCW3
9ipq09k7XQ

DataDash
https://www.youtube.com/channel/UCCatR7nWbYrkVXdxXb
4cGXw/videos

Legit Crypto
https://www.youtube.com/user/YourLegitGamingVids/videos

The Big Beesy
https://www.youtube.com/channel/UCDxK2PwEDvoaHZgjPV
_WgcA

The Modern Investor https://www.youtube.com/channel/UC-
5HLi3buMzdxjdTdic3Aig

Yes4motivation
https://www.youtube.com/user/sliceandice08/videos

Understanding technology

Ivan on Tech –
https://www.youtube.com/channel/UCrYmtJBtLdtm2ov84ulV-
yg

Price predictions with technical analysis

Crypto Espi
https://www.youtube.com/channel/UCIG0J8zd9N0XZzq_gJ3K
Waw/videos

Naeem Al-Obaidi
https://www.youtube.com/user/snipers/videos

XRP news

Alex Cobb
https://www.youtube.com/channel/UCg5GzcNQp5C6STqLP9
vNAow/videos

CKJ Crypto News
https://www.youtube.com/channel/UCmexsZ6pFvmXa9hOnny
Rz5A/videos

Crpto Eri
https://www.youtube.com/user/erichanintokyo/videos

Digital Asset Investor
https://www.youtube.com/channel/UCtQycmSrKdJ0zE0bWum
O4vA/videos

Esoteric Trading Solutions Teaching Crypto Markets
https://www.youtube.com/channel/UC70Q-2uXkC_5xk9
L5qhm1Q/videos

Jungle Inc
https://www.youtube.com/channel/UC9t0DRLy5_dQEpb8nPK
AiQA/videos

Love for Crypto https://www.youtube.com/channel/UCNx_o-
lrpiA2lA1OnMKqb_A/videos

Thinking Crypto
https://www.youtube.com/channel/UCjpkwsuHgYx9fBE0ojs
J_-w

EOS news

Crypto Tim
https://www.youtube.com/user/Timosborn7/videos

Cypherglass
https://www.youtube.com/channel/UCnXofUeO5w1dO9JGW
WDdqPQ

Dallas Rushing
https://www.youtube.com/channel/UCMiOtNUmlOO0V01wX
K8p0Kg

EOS San Diego https://www.youtube.com/channel/UC0J
dSIBvRyXtuurG97i4NQ/videos

Eos Tips https://www.youtube.com/channel/UC
pGtazr7k8HG_Sge6s_lbw/videos

Investing with a difference
https://www.youtube.com/channel/UC6SxkB3kM4uNs_yIU0L
qo_w
The Awakenment
https://www.youtube.com/channel/UCMiOtNUmlOO0V01wX
K8p0Kg
Wickedly Crypto https://www.youtube.com/channel/UCe
b1b8N528FzhQjQSHjbAw/videos

Forums

I prefer Youtube, but that's just me. If you want to talk about crypto, below is a list of forums:

- o Telegram
- o XRP Chat
- o Bitcointalk
- o Cryptocurrency Talk
- o Twitter
- o Steemit
- o Reddit
- o Stack Exchange
- o Investing.com

Bibliography

Allison, I., 2017. *Blockchain-based Ubitquity pilots with Brazil's land records bureau.* [Online] Available at: https://www.ibtimes.co.uk/blockchain-based-ubitquity-pilots-brazils-land-records-bureau-1615518
[Accessed December 2018].

Amadeo, K., 2018. *AIG Bailout, cost, timeline, bonuses, causes, effects.* [Online] Available at: https://www.thebalance.com/aig-bailout-cost-timeline-bonuses-causes-effects-3305693 [Accessed December 2018].

Ambisafe, n.d. *Smart Contracts: 10 Use Cases for Business.* [Online] Available at: https://ambisafe.com/blog/smart-contracts-10-use-cases-business/ [Accessed December 2018].

American Express, 2017. *American Express Introduces Blockchain-Enabled Cross-Border Business-to-Business Payments.* [Online] Available at: https://about.americanexpress.com/press-release/american-express-introduces-blockchain-enabled-cross-border-business-business
[Accessed December 2018].

Arnold, A., 2018. *How Institutional Investors Are Changing The Cryptocurrency Market.* [Online] Available at: https://www.forbes.com/sites/andrewarnold/2018/10/19/how-institutional-investors-are-changing-the-cryptocurrency-market/#4b55efa01ffe [Accessed December 2018].

Attkisson, S., 2009. *Where did the bailout billions really go?.* [Online] Available at: https://www.cbsnews.com/news/where-did-the-bailout-billions-really-go/

Bardinelli, J., 2018. *Top 100 Cryptocurrencies in 10 Words or Less.*
[Online] Available at: https://www.investinblockchain.com/top-100-
cryptocurrencies-10-words/ [Accessed December 2018].

Bartash, J., 2018. *Here's who owns a record $21.21 trillion of US debt.*
[Online] Available at: https://www.marketwatch.com/story/heres-who-
owns-a-record-2121-trillion-of-us-debt-2018-08-21
[Accessed December 2018].

Bitcoin Exchange Guide News Team, 2018. *Israel Seeks to Become Global
Crypto and Blockchain Innovation Leader.* [Online] Available at:
https://bitcoinexchangeguide.com/israel-seeks-to-become-global-crypto-
and-blockchain-innovation-leader/62[Accessed December 2018].

Bland, B., 2007. *BNP freezes funds in sub-prime shock.* [Online]
Available at: https://www.telegraph.co.uk/finance/markets/2813757/BNP-
freezes-funds-in-sub-prime-shock.html [Accessed December 2018].

Bowers, J. T. a. S., 2011. *RBS failure caused by 'multiple poor decisions',.*
[Online] Available at:
https://www.theguardian.com/global/2011/dec/12/royal-bank-of-scotland-
fsa-report [Accessed December 2018].

BrendanBlumer, 2019. *BrendanBlumer.* [Online] Available at:
https://twitter.com/BrendanBlumer/status/1080164179091193857
[Accessed January 2019].

Buchko, S., 2018. *https://coincentral.com/ethereum-vs-eos/.* [Online]
Available at: https://coincentral.com/ethereum-vs-eos/
[Accessed December 2018].

Buck, J., 2017. *Digital Currency Dash Now Usable at 13,000 Locations In
Brazil.* [Online] Available at: https://cointelegraph.com/news/digital-

currency-dash-now-usable-at-13000-locations-in-brazil [Accessed December 2018].

Canellis, D., 2018. *China brags its cryptocurrency ban has practically killed local Bitcoin trading Blockchains are totally okay, though.* [Online] Available at: https://thenextweb.com/hardfork/2018/07/09/china-crackdown-bitcoin/ [Accessed December 2018].

Cant, J., 2018. *Craig Wright threatens to send Bitcoin price down to $1,000, while BTC dumps.* [Online] Available at: https://www.chepicap.com/en/news/5189/craig-wright-threatens-to-send-bitcoin-price-down-to-1000-while-btc-dumps.html [Accessed December 2018].

Castillo, M. d., 2017. *Brazil's Central Bank is ramping up blockchain.* [Online] Available at: https://brazilcham.com/articles/brazils-central-bank-ramping-blockchain-rd [Accessed December 2018].

Chandler, S., 2018. *How Venezuela Came to Be One of the Biggest Markets for Crypto in the World.* [Online] Available at: https://cointelegraph.com/news/how-venezuela-came-to-be-one-of-the-biggest-markets-for-crypto-in-the-world [Accessed December 2018].

Chang, L., 2017. *Smartphone adoption will soon match total population in Brazil.* [Online] Available at: https://www.digitaltrends.com/mobile/brazil-smartphone-adoption-population/ [Accessed December 2018].

Christopher Bendiksen, S. G. a. E. L., 2018. *The Bitcoin mining network – Trends, Marginal creation cost, electricity consumption & sources.* [Online] Available at: chrome-extension://oemmndcbldboiebfnladdacbdfmadadm/ https://coinshares.co.uk/wp-content/uploads/2018/11/Mining-Whitepaper-Final.pdf [Accessed December 2018].

Cobb, A., 2018. *MoneyTap Is Now Live and Has The Potential To Utilize XRP In The Future.* [Online] Available at: https://www.youtube.com/watch?v=qajbKaEjYM8 [Accessed December 2018].

Coinmarketcap, 2013. *Historical Snapshot - April 28, 2013.* [Online] Available at: https://coinmarketcap.com/historical/20130428/ [Accessed December 2018].

cointelegraph.com, 2018. *Airfox Launches Mobile App in Brazil, Giving Unbanked Citizens Access to Previously Inaccessible Financial Services.* [Online] Available at: https://cointelegraph.com/press-releases/airfox-launches-mobile-app-in-brazil [Accessed December 2018].

Cuthbertson, A., 2018. *Bitcoin is 'better' and 'more stable' than gold and the US dollar.* [Online] Available at: https://www.independent.co.uk/life-style/gadgets-and-tech/news/bitcoin-steve-wozniak-blockchain-apple-cryptocurrency-revolution-a8357336.html [Accessed December 2018].

Cypherglass, 2018. *Usability on the EOS Network.* [Online] Available at: https://www.youtube.com/watch?v=ws95EZtdEOQ [Accessed December 2018].

CyptoTim, 2018. *https://www.youtube.com/watch?v=pVM-MqZGsTY.* [Online] Available at: https://www.youtube.com/watch?v=pVM-MqZGsTY [Accessed December 2018].

De, N., 2018. *Fidelity Is Launching a Crypto Trading Platform.* [Online] Available at: https://www.coindesk.com/fidelity-reveals-cryptocurrency-and-digital-asset-trading-platform [Accessed December 2018].

Dixit, K., 2018. *Ripple tests to extend till 14th Feb says Woori and Shinhan.* [Online] Available at: https://ambcrypto.com/ripple-tests-extend-till-14th-feb-says-woori-shinhan/ [Accessed December 2018].

Emem, M., 2018. *Japanese Government to Simplify Cryptocurrency Taxation Process.* [Online] Available at: https://www.ccn.com/japanese-government-to-simplify-cryptocurrency-taxation-process/ [Accessed December 2018].

EOS Tips, 2018. *How To Earn Interest On Your EOS Tokens Using Chintai.* [Online] Available at: https://www.youtube.com/watch?v=tf6mCfDHIoQ&t=0s&list=LLJx0-Hh2xRpD_biEwQA0fhg&index=2 [Accessed December 2018].

Frumkin, D., 2018. *The Top 20 Ethereum Tokens.* [Online] Available at: https://www.investinblockchain.com/top-ethereum-tokens/ [Accessed December 2018].

Global Findex, 2017. *Global Findex.* [Online] Available at: chrome-extension://oemmndcbldboiebfnladdacbdfmadadm/https://globalfindex.worldbank.org/sites/globalfindex/files/countrybook/India.pdf [Accessed December 2018].

Hamilton, D., 2018. *Japan & Crypto – Lessons in Blockchain Regulation.* [Online] Available at: https://coincentral.com/japan-crypto-lessons-in-blockchain-regulation/ [Accessed December 2018].

Hankin, A., 2018. *Here's how much it costs to mine a single bitcoin in your country.* [Online] Available at: https://www.marketwatch.com/story/heres-how-much-it-costs-to-mine-a-single-bitcoin-in-your-country-2018-03-06 [Accessed December 2018].

Hay, S., 2018. *Complete list of Bitcoin friendly countries for cryptocurrency businesses in 2018.* [Online] Available at: https://99bitcoins.com/bitcoin-friendly-countries/ [Accessed December 2018].

Helms, K., 2018. *Japan Introduces New Screening Requirements for Crypto Exchanges.* [Online] Available at: https://news.bitcoin.com/japan-screening-requirements-crypto-exchanges/ [Accessed December 2018].

HMRC, 2018. *Policy paper Cryptoassets for individuals.* [Online] Available at: https://www.gov.uk/government/publications/tax-on-cryptoassets/cryptoassets-for-individuals#which-taxes-apply [Accessed December 2018].

Horsley, S., 2007. *Adjustable-Rate Mortgages Fuel Foreclosure Crisis.* [Online] Available at: https://www.npr.org/templates/story/story.php?storyId=14218075 [Accessed December 2018].

Huang, Z., 2018. *Bitcoin cash "hard fork": everything you need to know about the latest cryptocurrency civil war.* [Online] Available at: https://www.scmp.com/tech/blockchain/article/2173389/bitcoin-cash-hard-fork-everything-you-need-know-about-latest [Accessed December 2018].

Huillet, M., 2018. *R3 Adds Ripple as First Crypto for Its Universal Payments DApp.* [Online] Available at: https://cointelegraph.com/news/r3-adds-ripple-as-first-crypto-for-its-universal-payments-dapp [Accessed December 2018].

Invest in blockchain, 2018. *Cryptocurrencies In The Top 100 With Working Products That Are In-Use.* [Online] Available at: https://www.investinblockchain.com/top-cryptocurrencies-working-products/ [Accessed December 2018].

Karmin, C., 2013. *Blackstone to buy stakes in apartment complexes from GE unit.* [Online] Available at: https://www.wsj.com/articles/blackstone-to-buy-stakes-in-apartment-complexes-from-ge-unit-1376338760?tesla=y [Accessed December 2018].

Kramer, M., 2018. *Ethereum Casper Update Expected in 2019, Sharding in 2020.* [Online] Available at: https://unhashed.com/cryptocurrency-news/ethereum-sharding-update-expected-2020/ [Accessed December 2018].

Lanz, J., 2018. *Mexican Presidential Candidate Plans to Fight Corruption With Blockchain Tech.* [Online] Available at: https://cryptoslate.com/mexican-presidential-candidate-plans-to-fight-corruption-with-blockchain-tech/ [Accessed December 2018].

ledger.com, 2019. *Supported Crypto Assets.* [Online] Available at: https://www.ledger.com/pages/supported-crypto-assets?r=c06d&tracker=CSBP [Accessed January 2019].

Lielacher, A., 2018. *The Top Five Ethereum Competitors.* [Online] Available at: https://btcmanager.com/the-top-five-ethereum-competitors/ [Accessed December 2018].

Macdonald, A., 2018. *EOS Vs Ethereum: Predicting The Winner Of The Smart Contract War.* [Online] Available at: https://cryptobriefing.com/eos-ethereum-smart-contract-war-winner/ [Accessed December 2018].

Mail, H. T. f. T. D., 2017. *Ten years on... Millions still paying the price of Northern Rock collapse: How the financial crisis robbed pensioners of half of their income.* [Online] Available at: https://www.thisismoney.co.uk/money/news/article-4877618/Financial-crisis-robbed-pensioners-half-income.html [Accessed December 2018].

Malwa, S., 2018. *Mexican Government Introduces Laws for Crypto Exchanges.* [Online] Available at: https://cryptoslate.com/mexican-government-introduces-laws-for-crypto-exchanges/ [Accessed December 2018].

Mangal, A., 2018. *What is OmiseGO? A Comprehensive Guide.* [Online] Available at: https://coincentral.com/what-is-omisego/ [Accessed December 2018].

Mari, A., 2017. *Brazilian fintech Nubank aims for the country's unbanked.* [Online] Available at: https://www.zdnet.com/article/brazilian-fintech-nubank-aims-for-the-countrys-unbanked/ [Accessed December 2018].

Marinoff, N., 2018. *Bitmain Nears 51% of Network Hash Rate: Why This Matters and Why It Doesn't.* [Online] Available at: https://bitcoinmagazine.com/articles/bitmain-nears-51-network-hash-rate-why-matters-and-why-it-doesnt/ [Accessed December 2018].

Marquer, S., 2017. *XRP Ledger Decentralizes Further With Expansion to 55 Validator Nodes.* [Online] Available at: https://ripple.com/insights/xrp-ledger-decentralizes-expansion-55-validator-nodes/ [Accessed December 2018].

Marquer, S., 2019. *XRP Ledger Decentralizes Further With Expansion to 55 Validator Nodes.* [Online] Available at: https://ripple.com/insights/xrp-ledger-decentralizes-expansion-55-validator-nodes/ [Accessed January 2019].

Mathew, R., 2018. *SWIFT GPI vs Ripple Payments.* [Online] Available at: https://www.finextra.com/blogposting/16147/swift-gpi-vs-ripple-payments [Accessed December 2018].

Maurya, N., 2018. *US Regulators in Splits over the Future of Cryptocurrency as CFTC Chief States "Crypto are here to stay".* [Online]

Available at: https://coingape.com/cftc-chief-crypto-are-here-to-stay/ [Accessed December 2018].

Nakamoto, S., 2008. *Bitcoin: A Peer-to-Peer Electronic Cash System.* [Online] Available at: https://bitcoin.org/bitcoin.pdf

Narayanan, A., 2018. *Written Testimony of Arvind NarayananAssociate Professor of Computer Science, Princeton University, United States Senate, Committee on Energy and Natural ResourcesHearing on Energy Efficiency of Blockchain and Similar Technologies.* [Online] Available at: chrome-extension://oemmndcbldboiebfnladdacbdfmadadm/https://www.energy.se nate.gov/public/index.cfm/files/serve?File_id=8A1CECD1-157C-45D4-A1AB-B894E913737D [Accessed December 2018].

News, B., 2018. *RBS bailout 'unlikely to be recouped'.* [Online] Available at: https://www.bbc.co.uk/news/business-45500384 [Accessed December 2018].

Nguyen, P. K. a. D., 2018. *The Bailout Scorecard.* [Online] Available at: https://projects.propublica.org/bailout/ [Accessed November 2018].

O'Keeffe, D., 2018. *Understanding Cryptocurrency Transaction Speeds.* [Online] Available at: https://medium.com/coinmonks/understanding-cryptocurrency-transaction-speeds-f9731fd93cb3 [Accessed December 2018].

O'Neal, S., 2018. *From Qatar to Palestine: How Cryptocurrencies Are Regulated in the Middle East.* [Online] Available at: https://cointelegraph.com/news/from-qatar-to-palestine-how-cryptocurrencies-are-regulated-in-the-middle-east [Accessed December 2018].

Pollock, D., 2018. *Story of Coincheck: How to Rebound After the 'Biggest Theft in the History of the World'.* [Online] Available at:

https://cointelegraph.com/news/story-of-coincheck-how-to-rebound-after-the-biggest-theft-in-the-history-of-the-world [Accessed December 2018].

Rao, P., 2018. *Africa could be the next frontier for cryptocurrency.* [Online] Available at: https://www.un.org/africarenewal/magazine/april-2018-july-2018/africa-could-be-next-frontier-cryptocurrency [Accessed December 2018].

Reporting by Cezary Podkul. Produced by Gabriel Gianordoli, J. K. T. P. P. S. a. H. S., 2018. *10 Years after the crisis.* [Online] Available at: http://graphics.wsj.com/how-the-world-has-changed-since-2008-financial-crisis [Accessed December 2018].

Review, E. o. A. B., 2018. *The number of cryptocurrency exchanges in Korea keeps growing despite recession.* [Online] Available at: https://www.asiablockchainreview.com/the-number-of-cryptocurrency-exchanges-in-korea-keeps-growing-despite-recession/ [Accessed December 2018].

Rooney, K., 2018. *Nasdaq plows ahead to launch bitcoin futures despite cryptocurrencies' bear market.* [Online] Available at: https://www.cnbc.com/2018/11/28/nasdaq-to-launch-bitcoin-futures-despite-cryptocurrencies-bear-market.html [Accessed December 2018].

Rooney, K., 2018. *Stock brokerage giant TD Ameritrade bets on a new cryptocurrency exchange.* [Online] Available at: https://www.cnbc.com/2018/10/03/td-ameritrade-bets-on-a-new-cryptocurrency-exchange.html [Accessed December 2018].

Rowley, J., 2017. *How Ethereum became the platform of choice for ICO'd digital assets.* [Online] Available at: https://techcrunch.com/2017/06/08/how-ethereum-became-the-platform-of-choice-for-icod-digital-assets/ [Accessed December 2018].

Said, C., 2003. *SPOTLIGHT / Chris Larsen: Puts the clout behind state's new privacy bill.* [Online] Available at: https://www.sfgate.com/business/article/SPOTLIGHT-Chris-Larsen-Puts-the-clout-behind-2594627.php [Accessed December 2018].

Shukla, A., 2018. *Bitcoin on highway to being legit.* [Online] Available at: http://www.newindianexpress.com/business/2018/dec/26/bitcoin-on-highway-to-being-legit-1916541.amp [Accessed December 2018].

Six Group, 2018. *SIX announcing fully end-to-end and fully integrated digital asset trading, settlement and custody service.* [Online] Available at: https://www.six-group.com/en/site/digital-exchange.html [Accessed December 2018].

Statista, 2018. *Number of registered Kik Messenger users worldwide from November 2012 to May 2016 (in millions).* [Online] Available at: https://www.statista.com/statistics/327312/number-of-registered-kik-messenger-users/ [Accessed December 2018].

Sunderland, H. S. a. R., 2008. *Credit crunch costs pension funds $5trn.* [Online] Available at: https://www.theguardian.com/money/2008/dec/14/pensions-credit-crunch-losses [Accessed December 2018].

Szabo, N., 1994. *Smart Contracts.* [Online] Available at: http://www.fon.hum.uva.nl/rob/Courses/InformationInSpeech/CDROM/Literature/LOTwinterschool2006/szabo.best.vwh.net/smart.contracts.html [Accessed December 2018].

The Awakenment , 2018. *How EOS is creating its own Economy + Update to Blockchain Real Estate.* [Online] Available at: https://www.youtube.com/watch?v=MsuruMDM22I [Accessed December 2018].

The Awakenment, 2017. *EOS = Blockchain Real Estate. How the price of EOS tokens will increase over time.* [Online] Available at: https://www.youtube.com/watch?v=svYvTkABDvo [Accessed December 2018].

The Korea Herald/Asia News Network, 2016. *A look at 5 richest conglomerate families in South Korea.* [Online] Available at: http://www.asiaone.com/business/look-5-richest-conglomerate-families-south-korea [Accessed 2018 December].

The Modern Investor, 2018. *Ethereum Raiden Network "Alpha" Is Active - 1 Million Transactions Per Second.* [Online] Available at: https://www.youtube.com/watch?v=vlY9s5ThXEE [Accessed December 2018].

The World Bank, 2017. *Remittances to Recover Modestly After Two Years of Decline.* [Online] Available at: http://www.worldbank.org/en/news/press-release/2017/10/03/remittances-to-recover-modestly-after-two-years-of-decline [Accessed December 2018].

Thomson Reuters, 2017. *Cryptocurrencies by country.* [Online] Available at: https://blogs.thomsonreuters.com/answerson/world-cryptocurrencies-country/ [Accessed December 2018].

Thomson, G., 2018. *Argentina – A Host Nation For Cryptocurrency.* [Online] Available at: https://cryptocoin.news/analysis/argentina-a-host-nation-for-cryptocurrency-16066/ [Accessed December 2018].

Trustnodes, 2018. *Ethereum's Ecosystem Estimated at 200,000 Developers with Truffle Seeing 80,000 Downloads a Month.* [Online] Available at: https://www.trustnodes.com/2018/07/22/ethereumsecosystem-estimated-200000-developers-truffle-seeing-80000-downloads-month [Accessed December 2018].

Velu, S., 2018. *How To Keep Your Cryptocurrency Safe: 7 Must Have Wallets.* [Online] Available at: https://blockgeeks.com/cryptocurrency-safe/ [Accessed January 2019].

Ver, R., 2018. *Roger Ver's Thoughts on 15th November Bitcoin Cash Upgrade.* [Online] Available at: https://www.youtube.com/watch?v=rFU1o-0oU7A [Accessed December 2018].

VK, A., 2018. *Ripple partner Santander says xCurrent-based OnePay FX satisfies "pent-up demand".* [Online] Available at: https://ambcrypto.com/ripple-partner-santander-says-xcurrent-based-onepay-fx-satisfies-pent-up-demand/ [Accessed December 2018].

Walters, S., 2018. *XRP News: Ripple Rolls Out XCurrent V4.0 Which Allows For Integration With XRapid.* [Online] Available at: https://www.investinblockchain.com/ripple-xcurrent-v4/ [Accessed December 2018].

Wellisz, C., 2018. *Digital Crusaders Technology offers weapons for the battle against corruption.* [Online] Available at: https://www.imf.org/external/pubs/ft/fandd/2018/03/wellisz.htm [Accessed December 2018].

Yang, J., 2018. *Thailand is becoming a critical country for blockchain.* [Online] Available at: https://techcrunch.com/2018/08/31/thailand-blockchain/?guccounter=1 [Accessed December 2018].

Young, J., 2018. *$80 Billion Banco Santander Uses Ripple For Payments, Will Many Banks Follow?.* [Online] Available at: https://www.ccn.com/80-billion-banco-santander-uses-ripple-for-payments-will-many-banks-follow/ [Accessed December 2018].

Young, J., 2018. *How South Korea's second-largest bank invested in a crypto exchange and shook up the market.* [Online] Available at: https://www.theblockcrypto.com/2018/11/23/how-south-koreas-second-largest-bank-invested-in-a-crypto-exchange-and-shook-up-the-market/ [Accessed December 2018].

Young, J., 2018. *South Korean Officials Prohibited From Holding or Trading Cryptocurrency.* [Online] Available at: https://www.ccn.com/south-korean-officials-prohibited-holding-trading-cryptocurrency/ [Accessed December 2018].

Young, J., 2018. *Vitalik Buterin: Ethereum Will Eventually Achieve 1 Million Transactions Per Second.* [Online] Available at: https://www.ccn.com/vitalik-buterin-ethereum-will-eventually-achieve-1-million-transactions-per-second/ [Accessed December 2018].